NATURE'S CHILDREN

HUMMINGBIRDS

by Josh Gregory

Children's Press®

An Imprint of Scholastic Inc.

Content Consultant
Dr. Stephen S. Ditchkoff
Professor of Wildlife Ecology and Management
Auburn University
Auburn, Alabama

Photographs ©: cover: Martin Mecnarowski/Shutterstock, Inc.;
1: Steffen Foerster/Dreamstime; 2 background: Jinyoung Lee/
Dreamstime; 2 hummingbird: Martin Ellis/Dreamstime; 3 background:
Jinyoung Lee/Dreamstime; 3 hummingbird: Martin Ellis/Dreamstime;
4: Gea Strucks/Dreamstime; 5 background: Gea Strucks/Dreamstime;
5 top inset: Judy Bellah/Alamy Images; 5 bottom inset: Pimmimemom/
Dreamstime; 7: Martin Ellis/Dreamstime; 8: Kevin Elsby/FLPA/Science
Source; 11: Ondrej Prosicky/Shutterstock, Inc.; 12: Gea Strucks/
Dreamstime; 15: Steve Gettle/Getty Images; 16: Judy Bellah/Alamy
Images; 19: Max Allen/Alamy Images; 20: DiaMartori/iStockphoto;
23: Mark Thomas/Alamy Images; 24: Kelly Nelson/Dreamstime; 27:
All Canada Photos/Alamy Images; 28: Barcroft/Getty Images; 31:
Vilainecrevette/Dreamstime; 32: FANTHOMME Hubert/Getty Images;
35: Gallinagomedia/Dreamstime; 36: Pimmimemom/Dreamstime; 39:
Marin Shields/Getty Images; 40: Glenn Bartley/BIA/Getty Images;
44 background: Jinyoung Lee/Dreamstime; 45 background: Jinyoung
Lee/Dreamstime; 46: Steffen Foerster/Dreamstime.

Maps by Bob Italiano.

Library of Congress Cataloging-in-Publication Data
Names: Gregory, Josh, author.
Title: Hummingbirds / by Josh Gregory.
Other titles: Nature's children (New York, N.Y.)
Description: New York : Children's Press, an imprint of Scholastic Inc.,
    [2017] | Series: Nature's children | Includes bibliographical
    references and index.
Identifiers: LCCN 2015043581| ISBN 9780531230299 (library
binding) | ISBN 9780531219355 (pbk.)
Subjects: LCSH: Hummingbirds—Juvenile literature.
Classification: LCC QL696.A558 G74 2017 | DDC 598.7/64—dc23
LC record available at http://lccn.loc.gov/2015043581

Printed in China 62
SCHOLASTIC, CHILDREN'S PRESS, and associated logos are
trademarks and/or registered trademarks of Scholastic Inc.

1 2 3 4 5 6 7 8 9 10 R 26 25 24 23 22 21 20 19 18 17

Hummingbirds

Class	Aves
Order	Apodiformes
Family	Trochilidae
Genera	102 genera
Species	328 species
World distribution	North, Central, and South America
Habitats	Rain forests, deserts, mountains, plains
Distinctive physical characteristics	Ranges in length from about 2.2 to 8 inches (5.6 to 20 centimeters), including beak and tail; ranges in weight from about 0.07 to 0.71 ounces (2 to 20 grams); females are often slightly larger than males; males have brightly colored feathers and may display crests, longer tail feathers, or other decorations; legs are small and weak; beak is long and very narrow, with a slight downward curve
Habits	Active during the day; spends most of its time perched to preserve energy; almost never walks, even for very short distances; enters a state of torpor at night to conserve energy; some species migrate up to 3,000 miles (4,828 kilometers) annually during the spring and fall; some species are territorial and will chase other hummingbirds or even other species away from food sources
Diet	Mostly nectar; also eats insects and spiders

Contents

CHAPTER 1

Zooming through the Sky

Out in the backyard garden, sunlight shines down on the many colorful flowers you helped your parents plant. There are red ones, purple ones, yellow ones—almost every color you can think of. As you look at these beautiful plants, you notice a small animal flying from flower to flower. It zips from one location to another in the blink of an eye. You can hear a low buzzing sound when it flies in your direction. Is it some sort of large insect?

Taking a closer look, you notice that the creature is covered in feathers. A bright red patch on its neck especially stands out. Above that, you can see its long beak. It's a bird! At first, you can't believe it. You've never seen a bird that was so tiny or that flapped its wings so fast. This isn't just any bird, though. It's a ruby-throated hummingbird.

Male ruby-throated hummingbirds have red feathers at their necks, but females do not.

Tiny Birds

Hummingbirds are famous for their small size. The smallest **species** of all is the bee hummingbird. It is found on the island nation of Cuba in the Caribbean Sea. This tiny creature is not only the smallest hummingbird but also the smallest of all birds living today. From the tip of its long beak to the end of its tail, it measures just 2.2 inches (5.6 centimeters). It weighs only 0.07 ounces (2 grams). That is less than the weight of a single penny.

Even the largest hummingbirds aren't very big. The giant hummingbird of South America is the biggest hummingbird species alive. It is about 8 inches (20 cm) long and can fit easily in a person's hand. At 0.71 ounces (20 g), it weighs about 10 times as much as a bee hummingbird. However, this is still less than the weight of a small handful of coins.

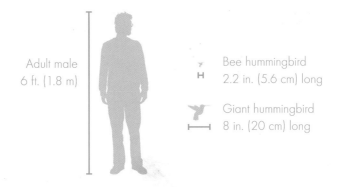

Adult male
6 ft. (1.8 m)

Bee hummingbird
2.2 in. (5.6 cm) long

Giant hummingbird
8 in. (20 cm) long

The tiny bee hummingbird is most common in the dense forests of Cuba.

Bright and Beautiful

In most hummingbird species, males and females look very different from each other. For one thing, females are generally a little bit larger than males. Females' feathers are often much duller colors, too.

In contrast, the feathers of male hummingbirds are among the most beautiful of all birds. They come in a wide variety of shiny colors. Blue and green are the most common. Many hummingbirds have feathers that are **iridescent**. This means they appear to change color when viewed from different angles. Many male hummingbirds have special, decorative feather arrangements. These make the birds stand out even more. Flashy features might include a **crest** on the bird's head or extra feathers on its legs that look somewhat like pants. Many male hummingbirds have colorful patches on their throats. They also may have extra-long tail feathers.

The males of some hummingbird species, such as the tufted coquette, have extra-long, brightly colored feathers on their head and neck.

Hummingbird Homes

Wild hummingbirds are found only in certain parts of North, Central, and South America. They are most common in South America. Of the 328 species around today, 23 are known to visit North America. Only 17 breed and live there regularly. More than half of them live in the South American countries of Brazil and Ecuador.

Hummingbirds can be found in a wide range of habitats. In terms of basic needs, as long as these birds have a place to perch and plenty of flowers nearby, they are happy. Different species are, however, particularly well suited to certain environments. There are hummingbirds that live in sandy deserts and hummingbirds that live in grassy plains. Some species can even be found thousands of feet above sea level in rocky mountain environments. Hummingbirds are most common in the tropical rain forests of South America. In these areas, the weather is warm all year and a wide variety of plant life is always available.

Desert-dwelling hummingbirds sometimes feed on cactus flowers.

CHAPTER 2

Speedy and Hungry

Hummingbirds are extremely fast fliers. The speediest species can rocket through the air at up to 30 miles per hour (48 kilometers per hour). When diving, they become even faster, reaching speeds above 50 miles per hour (80.5 kph). To achieve these incredible speeds, a hummingbird flaps its wings anywhere from 20 to 200 times per second. Small species flap faster, while large ones flap more slowly.

Most birds flap their wings up and down, propelling themselves up and forward on the downward flap. Nearly all their energy is spent when flapping down. Hummingbirds fly differently. Their strong muscles put large amounts of energy into flapping both up and down. They also rotate their wings in different directions. This enables them to move forward, backward, sideways, or straight up and down. They can switch direction in an instant. Hummingbirds can even fly upside down and hover in place. Because they are so skilled at flying, hummingbirds almost never walk. They fly even to travel very short distances along a branch.

Unlike other types of birds, a hummingbird can fly upside down.

Sipping Sweet Nectar

Roughly 90 percent of a hummingbird's diet is made up of a substance called nectar. This sweet, sugary liquid is produced in flowers. It is sometimes located inside a deep, narrow blossom. A hummingbird's long beak comes in handy for reaching this food. So do its flying abilities. To eat, a hummingbird hovers in front of a flower and sticks its beak inside. It then uses its long tongue to lick up the nectar. With this technique, it might drink up to 14 times its own weight in a single day.

Hummingbirds sometimes eat insects and spiders. They rely on their speed and **agility** to capture **prey**. When a hummingbird spots an insect to eat, it flies above it and dives down to snatch its prey. Hummingbirds can catch flying insects right in the air. This method of hunting is called hawking. A hummingbird might hawk such insects as wasps, ants, and flies.

FUN FACT! A hummingbird can drink nectar from up to 20 flowers per minute.

A hummingbird's tongue extends from its long, narrow beak.

A Mighty Metabolism

Hummingbirds have to eat a lot of food because their speedy little bodies require a lot of energy to function. Their hearts beat very quickly, and flapping their wings burns energy at a remarkable rate. Just to stay alive, hummingbirds must eat very often. Luckily, a hummingbird's **metabolism** is just as speedy as its movements. It takes just a few minutes for the bird's body to digest a meal and turn it into usable energy.

If such a high metabolism worked as hummingbirds slept, they would risk starving to death overnight. To avoid this, a hummingbird's body changes the way it functions. When a hummingbird settles down at night, its body goes into **torpor**. Body systems slow down, and temperature and heart rate decrease. This reduces the amount of energy the bird uses. However, it is not easy to wake up from such a deep sleep. It can take up to an hour for a hummingbird to become fully alert and active after waking up.

A hummingbird finds a safe branch where it can sleep without the risk of attacks from predators.

Summer and Winter

Because hummingbirds live in so many different habitats, they encounter a wide range of temperatures. However, they all need to stay warm to survive. For those living in areas such as deserts or tropical rain forests, this is not a problem. They are comfortable year-round in the warm weather. Other species have developed ways of dealing with the colder temperatures in their habitats. For example, those that live in snowy mountain homes might take shelter in caves or other protected areas at night.

Other hummingbird species migrate to avoid cold winter weather. This is especially common among hummingbirds in North America. Temperatures on that continent can change drastically between seasons. Some hummingbirds migrate very long distances. For example, the rufous hummingbird makes the journey back and forth between Mexico and Alaska every year. This route is 3,000 miles (4,828 km) each way. To prepare for the journey, migrating hummingbirds must eat extra food to gain body weight. This weight is burned off during the long flight.

Some hummingbirds are adapted to the dangerous cold of winter and others migrate to avoid it.

Small and Strong

Despite their small size, hummingbirds are not easy targets for **predators**. Many animals try to eat hummingbirds. Birds such as owls, falcons, and hawks can be a threat. So can bats and snakes. However, hummingbirds are much more agile than these predators and can match or even exceed their speed. They can dodge and change direction so quickly that almost nothing can keep up with them. Hummingbirds will even launch their own attacks when threats draw near. They dive down at their enemies and quickly dodge away. If other hummingbirds are nearby, they join in to chase the predator away.

As a result of their swift flying abilities, hummingbirds are usually only at risk when they are caught off guard. There are certain situations that can be particularly dangerous. Sometimes small hummingbirds fly into large spiderwebs and become caught. Other times, quick-moving frogs or praying mantises snatch them.

A hummingbird's amazing agility can help it escape from the clutches of a predator.

CHAPTER 3

Mates, Eggs, and Chicks

A hummingbird's daily routine begins early in the morning as the sun starts to rise. The bird slowly wakes from its torpor and waits for its body to warm up. It then searches for some nectar to eat. For the rest of the day, it will spend most of its time eating and perching. A hummingbird spends about 70 percent of its time perched. This helps it save energy. Hummingbirds also spend time taking baths every day. They get wet by splashing in puddles, showering in the rain, or even diving in and out of large bodies of water. Afterward, they **preen** to keep their feathers in good condition.

Hummingbirds are not very social. Many are even **territorial**. They perch where they can keep watch over their feeding area. This allows them to dive at other animals that come near. They do not attack only other hummingbirds. Larger birds, small mammals, and even humans can be targets for territorial hummingbirds.

Preening helps keep a hummingbird healthy.

Something to Say

Though they don't spend a lot of time socializing, hummingbirds can make a range of sounds to communicate. Each species has its own unique collection of calls. Most of the noises hummingbirds make are very high pitched. Some are short bursts of sound. Others are long and more complex. They might even sound like short songs. Some experts believe that the humming noises produced by the birds' rapidly flapping wings are a form of communication.

Communication serves several important purposes. For example, a hummingbird usually calls out before diving at an enemy. This alerts any nearby hummingbirds to the threat. Baby hummingbirds use a variety of calls to get their mother's attention. Some sounds indicate that they are hungry. Others let the mother know that her babies are in trouble. Calls can also be used to attract mates or warn away rivals.

Baby hummingbirds make noises to let their mother know what they want or need.

Showing Off

When it comes time to **mate**, male hummingbirds do their best to attract the attention of females. They put their colorful feathers on full display. Sometimes, they hover near a female and turn in all directions to show off their beautiful iridescent feathers. They might also perform complex displays of their flying abilities or sing special songs.

In some species, male hummingbirds form groups called leks when they are looking for mates. A lek can contain up to 100 males. Females visit leks when they are ready to mate. The males do their best to show off, and the females choose the ones they like best.

Male hummingbirds mate with as many females as they can. Females, on the other hand, choose a single mate each time they are ready to have babies. After mating, a female hummingbird begins building her nest. She uses materials such as plant parts, spiderwebs, and moss. Her mate does not help.

A male hummingbird performs a beautiful mating flight to impress a female.

Nesting and Nurturing

Female hummingbirds lay two eggs at a time. They lay the smallest eggs of any birds. The smallest hummingbird eggs are only the size of a pea. The largest aren't much larger than a marble. Still, the eggs are actually fairly large compared to the size of an adult hummingbird.

After laying her eggs, a female hummingbird sits on them to protect and warm them for 15 to 20 days. Then they are ready to hatch. After hatching, hummingbird chicks are blind and mostly naked. Their mother feeds them about twice each hour. She does this by **regurgitating** food directly into their mouths.

At first, the mother must continue sitting on her babies to keep them warm. By the time they are one to two weeks old, the babies have enough feathers to stay warm on their own. About two weeks after that, they are strong enough to start flying and finding their own food.

A mother hummingbird constructs a nest before laying her eggs.

CHAPTER 4

Hummingbird History

There are more than 10,000 different bird species living today. Hummingbirds make up only a small part of that number. From vultures to flamingos to owls to woodpeckers, these animals can have many differences between them. However, they all come from the same **ancestors**. Scientists believe that the earliest birds were close relatives of dinosaurs.

Though today they are found only in the Americas, hummingbirds probably first appeared in Europe and Asia. Scientists learned this by studying the **fossils** of ancient birds. They believe that the earliest hummingbird species first appeared about 42 million years ago. Over time, hummingbirds made their way from Europe into North America across a bridge of land that once connected the continents. As hummingbirds made their way into new habitats, they changed over time to meet the demands of their environments. This resulted in the many species we know today.

This hummingbird fossil dates back more than 30 million years.

Speedy Cousins

The closest living relatives of today's hummingbirds are a group of birds known as swifts. Together, hummingbirds and swifts make up the **order** Apodiformes. The word *Apodiformes* means "unfooted birds." This refers to the way these birds prefer to fly and almost never walk.

Swifts are a little larger than hummingbirds, but they are still among the smallest types of birds. Most of them measure between 3.5 and 9 inches (9 and 23 cm) long. Like hummingbirds, swifts are very fast flyers. Though they are not as agile as their tiny relatives, they can reach higher speeds than hummingbirds. Swifts regularly fly at up to 70 miles per hour (112.7 kph). They have been observed traveling even faster in short bursts.

One easy way to tell a swift apart from a hummingbird is to look at its beak. Unlike a hummingbird, a swift's beak is very short and wide. This is because swifts do not drink nectar from deep inside flowers. Instead, they fly around snatching insects out of the sky.

Swifts are named for their incredible speed.

CHAPTER 5

Humans and Hummingbirds

With their colorful feathers and incredible flying abilities, hummingbirds can be a lot of fun to watch. However, it is not always easy to spot them, even though hummingbirds often live in the same places humans do. Some people put feeders full of nectar-like sugar water in their yards or gardens to attract the birds. Others plant flowers that local hummingbird species like to feed on. People also visit zoos for the chance to see these beautiful birds up close.

In the past, many people tried to keep hummingbirds as pets. This is not good for hummingbirds, because they need plenty of space and access to flowers to stay healthy. People also hunted hummingbirds for their colorful feathers. They used these feathers as decorations on clothing and other objects. In the 1800s, this practice brought several hummingbird species close to extinction. Today, most people know that it is better to observe hummingbirds from a distance. Even so, some species remain endangered.

Several hummingbirds crowd around a feeder to eat.

Providing Plants with Pollen

Hummingbirds play an important role in keeping the environment healthy. Flowers provide the birds with a food source, and hummingbirds repay the flowers by helping them reproduce. Flowers produce a powdery substance called pollen. For these plants to make new seeds, the pollen must travel from one flower to another. Because plants cannot move around, they rely on animals to transfer pollen for them. As a hummingbird feeds on nectar from a flower, bits of pollen stick to its beak and feathers. When the bird flies to another flower, the pollen is transferred. The plant can then produce seeds so new plants can grow.

Hummingbirds help pollinate countless types of plants around the world. Some plants do not have any other animals to help them spread their pollen. This means that if hummingbirds died out, so would these plants.

This hummingbird has bits of pollen on its beak and head from its last meal.

Helping Hummingbirds Survive

Nine hummingbird species are critically endangered, and another 11 species are considered endangered. One major problem for hummingbird survival today is habitat destruction. Humans clear away natural land to make room for their own homes and businesses. Another issue is population fragmentation. This is when human development separates groups of hummingbirds from one another. Fragmentation makes it harder for hummingbirds to find mates and reproduce.

One way to help solve the problem of disappearing habitats is to plant plenty of flowers in yards, parks, and gardens. This allows hummingbirds to survive even as humans take up more and more space. It also brightens outdoor spaces with the natural beauty of flowers and these amazing birds. With a little help, hummingbirds will continue to make our world beautiful for a long time to come.

A red-tailed comet feeds on nectar from a flower in Bolivia.

Words to Know

agility (uh-JIL-uh-tee) — the ability to move quickly and easily

ancestors (AN-ses-turz) — ancient animal species that are related to modern species

crest (KREST) — a tuft of feathers on top of a bird's head

endangered (en-DAYN-jurd) — at risk of becoming extinct, usually because of human activity

extinction (ik-STINGK-shuhn) — the state of no longer being found alive

fossils (FAH-suhlz) — the hardened remains of prehistoric plants and animals

habitats (HAB-uh-tats) — places where an animal or a plant is usually found

iridescent (ir-ih-DES-uhnt) — shining with many different colors when seen from different angles

mate (MAYT) — to join together to produce babies

metabolism (muh-TAB-uh-liz-uhm) — the rate at which the body changes food into the energy needed to breathe, digest, and grow

migrate (MYE-grate) — to move to another area or climate at a particular time of year

order (OR-dur) — a group of related plants or animals that is bigger than a family but smaller than a class

perch (PURCH) — to sit or stand on the edge of something

pollen (PAH-luhn) — tiny yellow grains produced in the anthers of flowers

predators (PREH-duh-turz) — animals that live by hunting other animals for food

preen (PREEN) — to clean and arrange birds' feathers with their beaks

prey (PRAY) — an animal that is hunted by another animal for food

regurgitating (ri-GUR-ji-tayt-ing) — bringing food that has been swallowed back up to the mouth

species (SPEE-sheez) — one of the groups into which animals and plants of the same genus are divided

territorial (terr-uh-TOR-ee-uhl) — defensive of a certain area

torpor (TOR-pur) — a state of lowered physical activity that includes reduced metabolism, heart rate, breathing, and body temperature

Habitat Map

NORTH

AMERICA

PACIFIC

OCEAN

ATLANTIC

SOUTH
AMERICA

Hummingbird Range

ARCTIC OCEAN

EUROPE

ASIA

AFRICA

PACIFIC OCEAN

CEAN

INDIAN

OCEAN

AUSTRALIA

Find Out More

Books

Berne, Emma Carlson. *Hummingbirds: Faster Than a Jet!* New York: PowerKids Press, 2014.

Gish, Melissa. *Hummingbirds*. Mankato, MN: Creative Education, 2011.

Larson, Jeanette, and Adrienne Yorinks. *Hummingbirds: Facts and Folklore from the Americas*. Watertown, MA: Charlesbridge, 2011.

Sill, Cathryn P. *About Hummingbirds: A Guide for Children*. Atlanta: Peachtree, 2011.

Visit this Scholastic Web site for more information on hummingbirds:
www.factsfornow.scholastic.com
Enter the keyword **Hummingbirds**

Index

Page numbers in *italics* indicate a photograph or map.

About the Author

Josh Gregory is the author of more than 90 books for kids. He has written about everything from animals to technology to history. A graduate of the University of Missouri-Columbia, he currently lives in Portland, Oregon.